a special gift
for you

for

from

date

Karen Moore

Heart Strings

love is calling

B&H PUBLISHING GROUP

Nashville, Tennessee

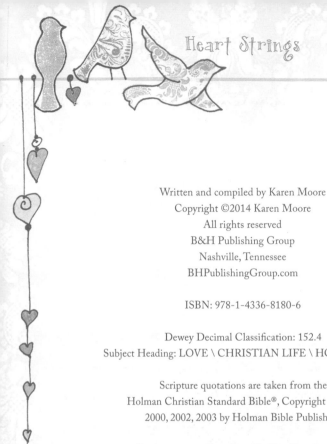

Heart Strings

Written and compiled by Karen Moore
Copyright ©2014 Karen Moore
All rights reserved
B&H Publishing Group
Nashville, Tennessee
BHPublishingGroup.com

ISBN: 978-1-4336-8180-6

Dewey Decimal Classification: 152.4
Subject Heading: LOVE \ CHRISTIAN LIFE \ HOLY SPIRIT

Scripture quotations are taken from the
Holman Christian Standard Bible®, Copyright ©1999,
2000, 2002, 2003 by Holman Bible Publishers.

Quotations are taken from *The New Encyclopedia of
Christian Quotations*, Copyright © 2000 John Hunt Publishing Ltd.
Published by Baker Books, a division of Baker Book House Company,
P.O. Box 6287, Grand Rapids, MI 49516-6287. All rights reserved.

Printed in China
1 2 3 4 5 6 17 16 15 14

Dedication

This book is dedicated to each person who has entered my life and taught me a little more about love. You've each tugged at my heartstrings and helped me become aware of the treasures love brings. You've helped me understand why we know God IS love!

May the Lord cause you to increase and overflow with love for one another and for everyone. (1 Thess. 3:12)

Welcome

Start the day with a little love. Embrace God's goodness! Fill your heart with grace and joy so that everyone you meet will feel the light of God's love all through the day.

Love really IS the answer and one that applies to every area of our lives. We can only know its true sweetness as we taste it through God's Spirit and let it radiate out from us to others. Love is the "pearl of great price," the clearest moment of connection, the deepest utterance of the heart.

Take a few moments then to start your day with love and let it carry you wherever you go. As one writer put it, "Love is the doorway through which the human soul passes from selfishness to service and from solitude to kinship with all mankind."

Open the door of your heart each day because love is always tied with heartstrings!

With Love in Christ,

Karen

Heart Strings

Born to Love

Therefore, as God's chosen ones, holy and loved, put on heartfelt compassion, kindness, humility, gentleness, and patience, accepting one another and forgiving one another if anyone has a complaint against another. Just as the Lord has forgiven you, so you must also forgive. (Col. 3:12–14)

When you were just a newcomer to the world, everything you knew about love came to you through your senses. Someone who loved you held you close when you were sleepy or needed comfort. They made sure you were bathed and fed and that you knew you were in a safe place. It was the beginning of what would blossom into your future understanding of love.

As time passed and you grew up, you learned to give love and to receive it in more ways. Little by little, string by string,

you became attached at the heart to those around you, those who would always be definitions of love to you.

You were designed to live in a world of love and to help others remember to love, and you were created by the Author of love and life itself.

Today and every day, you have a new chance to embrace love and offer a sense of it to everyone you meet. Nothing is sweeter than love tied gently with heartstrings.

Nothing is sweeter than love, nothing stronger, nothing higher, nothing wider, nothing more pleasant, nothing fuller or better in heaven or earth.
~ Thomas a Kempis

Love is always open arms. With arms open you allow love to come and go as it will, freely, for it'll do so anyway. If you close your arms about love, you'll find you are left only holding yourself.
~ Leo Buscaglia

Prayer:
Father, what a difference it makes
just knowing Your love and knowing
how much You want me to feel
loved. Thank You for the incredible
gift of love and help me to be willing
to share it in every good way. Amen.

Heart Strings

Love Is a Heart Thing!

We love because He first loved us.
(1 John 4:19)

Do you ever find yourself wondering about the whole concept of love? After all, we might say we love ice cream or we love playing volleyball. We might say we love our dog, checkers, or our shiny red Ford. We seem to "love" a lot of things.

How is it then that we use the same word when we talk about loving the people in our families, or loving our spouses? Sure the theologians can give us definitions for the kinds of love, agape, or brotherly love is quite different from romantic love. But there's more! Then there's God's love. Wow! Doesn't it seem awesome to know the God of the whole universe actually loved you first, that He knows you by name, and that He loves you beyond measure!!

Love is worth pondering, in all of its delightful forms, for each one is a matter of the heart and there are strings attached.

When I have learned to love God
    better than my earthly dearest,
I shall love my earthly dearest
    better than I do now.
~ C. S. Lewis

Words which do not
give the light of Christ
increase the darkness.
~ Mother Teresa

Only the heart knows how
to find what is precious!
~ Dostoevski

Prayer:
Lord, I'm not sure how You decided to create me and love me, but I'm grateful. Help me to reflect Your love to others and to love You right back. Amen.

Love Is Everywhere!

And we have come to know and to believe the love that God has for us. God is love, and the one who remains in love remains in God, and God remains in him. (1 John 4:16)

When we remember that our Creator God is always near, always present, and always ready to share His love with us, we know without a doubt that love is everywhere. We can feel it in the beautiful breeze of a warm, sunny day. We can taste it in the cup of tea shared with a friend. We can embrace it in the faces of neighbors and friends. God's love is everywhere.

It is beautiful to know that we are His ambassadors. We are the ones He counts on to continue to spread His love to others. He planted His children all around the globe for one reason …so that the whole world could come to know His love. What a glorious message to carry in your heart today!

A LITTLE STUDY OF THE HEART

See that your chief study be
  about your heart:
That there God's image may be planted
That there His interests be advanced
That there the world and flesh are subdued
That there the love of every sin is cast out.
That there the love of holiness grows.
  ~ Jonathan Edwards

To handle yourself, use your head.
To handle others, use your heart.
~ Unknown Writer

Prayer:
Father in heaven, it is truly amazing to think about Your love and to recognize it in the air we breathe and the ground we walk upon. We thank You that everywhere we turn, we can see the reflection of Your grace and power. Thank You for loving us so much. Amen.

Heart Strings

Love Is Always Calling!

Jesus said to them again, "Peace to you!
As the Father has sent Me, I also send you."
(John 20:21)

"Hello! This is love calling . . . God's love, that is! It would bring such joy to my heart to know that you have received me into your life, that you understand how much I love you."

If God could call us on the phone, or if "love" could text us, perhaps we'd get a message something like this one. Certainly God has been calling us since the day we were born and won't stop trying to get His message through every day we live.

We're His object of love and affection and nothing makes Him more pleased than knowing we have a strong relationship with Him.

He continually surrounds us with those people who have been sent into the world to proclaim His name and share His love. He doesn't want to miss any chance to draw you near to Him.

If His message comes through to you today, stop whatever you might be doing and answer the call. It will change your life!

The responsible person seeks to make his or her whole life a response to the question and call of God.
~ Dietrich Bonhoeffer

A CALL TO LOVE

I walked along the path of life, feeling
  rather small, when the King of all the
  Universe stopped me with His call.
He said, "I have some work to do and so
  you came to mind,
I need someone to light the way for those
  who are still blind.
I think you'd do the job quite well, but I'll
  give you the choice,
You can stay on your own path or listen to
  my voice."
So, then and there, I changed my course,
  sharing light and standing tall,
To bring prayer to others
  in answer to His call.
~Karen Moore

The awareness of a need
and the capacity to
meet that need:
this constitutes a call.
~John R. Mott

Prayer:
Lord, it's an awesome thing to realize how much effort You put into making sure we hear Your voice. You are willing to go wherever we are to give us another chance to answer Your call. Help us to open our ears and our hearts to You always. Amen.

Another Serving of Love

*Better a meal of vegetables where there is love
than a fattened ox with hatred. (Prov. 15:17)*

There's nothing quite as helpful to relationships as cooking up a little love together in the kitchen. Whether you invite the neighbors for Sunday dinner, or create a sumptuous pizza for two, you have a great opportunity to share a hearty meal of love.

Many of us love to share favorite recipes, or create specialty dishes for our friends. It gives us a source of sweet pride to share our delectable dishes and brings the chance to heal any wounds that may exist around the table. A dinner goes more smoothly when we serve big helpings of forgiveness and enjoy the gifts of our relationships.

The next time you sense a need for a generous and forgiving spirit to prevail, create an atmosphere of love by serving up your favorite recipes for joy, peace, and happiness. You'll find yourself at the heart of grace and laughter before you even get to dessert.

We pardon in the degree that we love.
~ La Rochfoucauld

It is idol for us to say
that we know God has
forgiven us if we are not loving
and forgiving ourselves.
~ Martin Lloyd-Jones

I NEED ANOTHER HELPING, GOD!

I'll take another helping,
In fact, please make it two,
'Cause I need your forgiveness
For the foolish things I do.
So forgive me with the first scoop
And then just like before,
Accept my sorry heart
And keep loving me some more.
Amen, Lord! Amen!
~Karen Moore

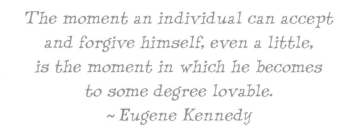

The moment an individual can accept
and forgive himself, even a little,
is the moment in which he becomes
to some degree lovable.
~ Eugene Kennedy

It is only with the
heart that one can see rightly,
what is essential
is invisible to the eye.
~Antoine de Saint Exupery

Prayer:
Lord, it's funny how a potluck or a simple dinner with kind words can change things. Help us to be more loving and more forgiving to each other. Give us a taste of Your divine forgiveness to sprinkle on all of our relationships. Amen.

Heart Strings

A Joyful Heart

A joyful heart makes a face cheerful, but a sad heart produces a broken spirit. (Prov. 15:13)

Need a heart transplant? Sometimes we've managed to get so far down in the doldrums that we hardly recognize all that is actually still right with the world. We look down at our feet and forget to look up at the stars!

If your life moves along the same lines as most of us, you have lots of ups and downs. The "downs" can become overwhelming and make your heart sad. They can cause your spirit to feel broken.

Remember this, though! God has overcome all the brokenness that this world can offer. He came to earth and brought us His radiant Light. This is not just the light of the world, but it's the light of your down days. It's the light that is meant to give you a reason to look up again and trust that better days are ahead.

If your heart is heavy today, then rest a while, and then lay your burdens at the feet of the One who loves you more than anything.

Humble yourselves, therefore, under the mighty hand of God, so that He may exalt you at the proper time, casting all your cares on Him, because He cares about you. (1 Pet. 5:6–7)

PEEKING THROUGH THE CLOUDS

If you need a little sunshine
'Cause it's a cloudy day,
But nothing that you do
Seems to chase those blues away,
Then lift your heart to Heaven
And say a little prayer,
For the God of Light and Sunshine
Will be sure to meet you there.
Then before you finish praying,
The gloom will disappear,
And you'll be blessed with joy
And a heart that's filled with cheer!
~Karen Moore

*Throw your heart over the fence
and the rest will follow.
~ Norman Vincent Peale*

Prayer:
Lord, there's nothing quite as
wonderful as the joy we feel when
springtime comes and all the earth
is alive again with fresh blossoms
and warm breezes. You know how
much our hearts need to feel free
like the wind, safe enough to run
and play and fill the day with laughter. Thank You for this kind of joy.
Amen.

The Beginning of Love

For now the winter is past; the rain has ended and gone away. The blossoms appear in the countryside. The time of singing has come, and the turtledove's cooing is heard in our land.
(Song of Songs 2:11–12)

Do you remember the first time you fell in love? You felt slightly dizzy, slightly befuddled about what to say or how to say it. Your heart raced like it had just been set free for the first time ever.

Love has a way of making everything seem different somehow. The world takes on a glow it didn't have before and your thoughts seem to carry you closer to the one you love every moment. You're awed, tickled, delighted beyond measure. Everything feels good.

Whenever you can, stop to remember the first blushing moments when you realized

31

you were in love and offer your heart again to the one you love now in a whole new way. Be excited! Be glad! Be blessed!

Let today be the beginning of a whole new love. Embrace the joy!

Let us make God the beginning and the end of our love, for he is the fountain from which all good things flow and into him alone they flow back. Let him therefore be the beginning of our love.
~ Richard Rolle

People are renewed by love. As sinful desire ages them, so love rejuvenates them.
~ Augustine of Hippo

Pursue love. (1 Cor. 14:1)

What's earth with all its art, verse, music, worth compared with love, found, gained and kept?
~ Robert Browning

Prayer:
Lord, thank You for each seed of love that You plant in our hearts. Thank You that each time we begin to love again, it helps us to grow stronger and more aware of others and of all You have done for us. Guard our hearts and our minds in Christ Jesus and help us to blossom in the love You've shown us. Amen.

What's Love Got to Do with It? Everything!

Do not owe anyone anything, except to love one another, for the one who loves another has fulfilled the law. (Rom. 13:8)

Have you ever noticed how easy it is to be in the presence of good friends, or of someone you love who loves you right back? Your relationship flourishes simply by being together, whether you're engaged in warm conversation, or simply co-existing in a peaceful and loving way. You don't have to think about it or explain it, or analyze it. You just get the blissful joy of being there.

Our relationship with God is like that too. When we are connected to Him in a comfortable way, we know that we can come together any time and feel at peace. We know nothing will be too big or too small to discuss, and that the love between us means that we're never alone!

Sometimes we get a little jaded about life and we even toss away the idea of genuine love, not realizing what it means and how it fulfills us. Our work then, is to be willing to allow love into our lives, to break through our uncertainty and help us to truly live in fullness. We may wonder at times what love has to do with anything.

The answer, the truth is beyond our understanding, but God is love, and love is everything!

Love is the fulfillment of all our works. There is the goal that is why we run: we run toward it, and once we reach it, in it we shall find rest.
~ Augustine of Hippo

The law of God and also the way of life is written in our hearts, it lies in no man's supposing, nor in any historical opinion, but in a good will and well doing.
~ Jacob Bohme

*Until he extends the circle of compassion
to include all living things,
man will not himself find peace.*
~ Albert Schweitzer

Prayer:
You know us so well, Father. You make sure we see Your love in all that surrounds us, that we feel Your presence, and know for sure You're there. Help us to never become so jaded in matters of love that we forget You are the source of all that love is meant to be, And that we can return to You for comfort at any time. Amen.

Heart Strings

Picking Daisies

My love is mine and I am his. (Song of Songs 2:16)

Did you ever pick a daisy and pull it's petals off one by one as you mused about love? "He loves me, he loves me not. He loves me, he loves me not." One by one those petals fell as you wondered whether the daisy would offer any insight into the relationship you were hoping for. Sure you were a mere teenager and any way of figuring out the answers in matters of love was appealing. Most of the time, you could even fudge the ending if the last petal was left with "He loves me not." After all, tomorrow was another day, or you simply may have picked the wrong daisy . . . you could just try again.

The daisies may not be able to tell you whether love exists or not, but your heart always will. Your heart will gather all the clues, all the moments and memories and pull them together in a garland of truth, a beautiful fragrant impression called love.

Pick a few daisies for the one you love today.

Love takes off masks that we fear
we cannot live without
and now we cannot live within.
~James Baldwin

The single desire that dominated
my search for delight was simply
to love and to be loved.
~Augustine of Hippo

Destiny is not a matter
of chance, it is a matter of choice;
it is not a thing to be waited for,
it is a thing to be achieved.
~ William J. Bryan

He who lives up to a little love
shall have more love.
~Thomas Brooks

Prayer:
Lord, thank You that we don't ever have to question whether or not You love us. Every daisy in Your garden has enough petals to always say, "He loves me." Nothing could mean more to your children than having that precious assurance. Amen.

Love ... Accept No Imitations!

Now the end of all things is near; therefore, be serious and disciplined for prayer. Above all, maintain an intense love for each other, since love covers a multitude of sins. (1 Pet. 4:7-8)

No matter what form of love you might want to talk about, one thing is true across the board. You can't fake love. You don't want an imitation. Love simply has to be authentic or it's nothing at all.

Of course, imitators are everywhere. You know the ones that pass as love for a time, even seem real for a while, but then can't sustain the lie, and so they simply fade away. If you need a way to gauge this for yourself, put God into the equation as your test case. Imagine how you'd feel if His love wasn't genuine? What if He was only pretending to love you? Where would you be?

43

Fortunately, God can never be anything but genuine and real. He is love. As human beings, we fall far short of that mark, but He loves us anyway. He says keep trying. Keep following My example and I'll help you get a sense, a better idea of what real love is all about.

Today we want nothing but honest, real, unvarnished relationships. We want to know that we can trust and enjoy the significant people in our lives. So, don't accept any imitations. Only go for the real thing!

You can never establish a personal
relationship without opening up your
own heart. ~ Paul Tournier

But imitate Christ, who is supremely
perfect and supremely holy,
and you will never err.
~ John of the Cross

We know the truth, not only by
the reason, but also by the heart.
~ Blaise Pascal

Whoever lives true life, will love true love.
~ Elizabeth Barrett Browning

Be so true to thyself,
as thou be not false to others.
~ Francis Bacon

Prayer:
There is no one like You, never has been, never will be. You are the genuine article, the original. All of us can only try to imitate You, try to come close to You in some way. Lord, help us to seek You with our whole hearts, minds, and souls. Help us to come to You with integrity. Amen.

Here's to Huggable You!

Greet one another with a holy kiss.
(1 Cor. 16:20)

Probably one of the best forms of communication for human beings anywhere is that warm, wonderful, wrap-me-up joy that comes with a hug. No matter where we live or who we are, we all can use a little extra love and there's nothing like a hug to make that possible.

It's reported that we need at least twelve hugs a day to simply stay reasonably balanced. Twelve hugs! Even if you're not keeping score, you probably fall well below the maintenance level hug quotient. Perhaps you could include dog or cat hugs, but we're primarily talking people hugs here.

You may remember a delightful poem by Shel Silverstein from his book, *Where the Sidewalk Ends*, called "Hug O' War." It's about how hugs are much better than tugs, because with giggles and grins, everyone wins.

47

Since you're an incredible hugger, this may be just the day to reach out and wrap your arms around someone special for no reason at all . . . well, perhaps just to say "you mean the world to me." Remember, no tugs, just hugs! Oh, don't you feel better already?

A hug and a squeeze
Is sure to please
Someone you love right now!
~Karen Moore

God has not created man to be a stick or stone but has given him five senses and a heart of flesh, so that he loves his friends, is angry with his enemies, and commiserates with his dear friends in adversity.
~ Martin Luther

Hardening of the heart ages people faster than hardening of the arteries.
~ Author Unknown

Whoever loves much, does much.
~ Thomas à Kempis

Prayer:
Lord, You are willing at any given moment to drop everything else and offer us comfort. You tuck us under Your wings and protect us from the things that hurt. You hug our hearts and bless us with each new sunrise. We reach up and send You our hugs right back. Amen.

49

faith and Love

*If I have all faith so that I can move mountains
but do not have love, I am nothing.
(1 Cor. 13:2)*

Sometimes we treat faith and love like they are just natural things that go together, like salt and pepper, or peanut butter and jam. Certainly, they do go together well, blended, mixed, stirred any way you can think of. Everything about them seems to work.

There's really only one catch to the faith and love recipe. For it to come out really well, it's best to have faith in the One who came up with the whole design and to accept His great love. From His love, all other love grows. From His work, faith matures.

Wherever you go today, sprinkle all you do with the blessing of faith and then send it on to the people around you with love. After all, together, they're a match made in heaven.

Now these three remain: faith, hope, and love.
But the greatest of these is love. (1 Cor. 13:13)

Love is an act of faith,
and whoever is of little faith
is also of little love.
~ Erich Fromm

It is the heart which is conscious
of God, not the reason.
This then is faith:
God is sensible to the heart,
not to the reason.
~ Blaise Pascal

Prayer:

Thank You, Lord, for having faith in us and for loving us so much. Forgive us when we step aside from our faith in You. Help us to come back quickly to be close to You and share in Your dreams for our lives. Amen.

Love Is Full of Possibility

With God all things are possible. (Matt. 19:26)

It may seem a bit cliché, but when we take a moment to recognize what love does as it comes into our lives, it's astounding. Love gives us new energy, new enthusiasm for the world around us, and a new sense that anything is possible. Love reminds us that we're valuable and that someone actually sees us and wants to have us near.

Imagine that feeling and then move to a new understanding of what it means to have God's love. His love draws you near, reminds you that you're valuable, and that through Him all things are possible. His love is the ultimate Source of all that brings you joy. His love is ever-present, always available. It is not conditional. It does not depend on whether you fulfilled your part of the relationship.

As in all relationships though, the more you share with Him, the more you can enjoy spending time together. The more you connect and communicate, the more you experience His love. His love makes all things possible!

55

Whom should we love, if not him who loved us,
and gave himself for us? If the bliss even of
angels and glorified souls, consists greatly in
seeing, and praising, the Son of God surely,
to love, to trust, and to celebrate the friend of
sinners, must be a principal ingredient
in the happiness of saints not yet made perfect.
~ Augustus Toplady

"If you have faith the size of
a mustard seed, you will tell this mountain,
'Move from here to there,' and it will move.
Nothing will be impossible for you."
(Matt. 17:20)

The nearer we draw to God in our love for him,
the more we are united together by love for our
neighbor and the greater our union with our
neighbor, the greater is our union with God.
~ Dorotheus of Gaza

Possible, Positive, Praiseworthy
Phenomenal God's Love!

Heart to heart
And strand by strand,
We're tied by heartstrings,
Hand to hand!
~Karen Moore

Prayer:
Father, no one loves me like You do.
No one gives me the possibility to
become more, to live more fully, and
to love more than You do. Thank
You for Your gifts to me. Amen.

Compassionate Hearts

The LORD is gracious and compassionate, slow to anger and great in faithful love. The LORD is good to everyone; His compassion rests on all He has made. (Ps. 145:8-9)

As human beings, as parents, friends, and neighbors, we've had plenty of opportunities to learn about compassion. We are almost overwhelmed with the needs of the world and with the needs of those in our own social circle. Of course, knowing how to be compassionate, sensing a need in those around us, and acting on those thoughts and feelings may be different things.

The Psalmist says that "The LORD is good to everyone; His compassion rests on all He has made." When you consider being more compassionate, does any one person or cause come to mind?

Is there any reason not to act on that urging of your heart?

We each have the opportunity to be "the good Samaritan," to be the person who does not walk by another in need, but who stops and offers to be the hands and feet of Jesus.

May your spirit guide you as you consider the ways to open up your heart to others and to lend a hand. After all, God may well have put you in that place and moment for that exact reason. You have such a good heart!

The best exercise for
strengthening the heart
is reaching down and lifting people up.
~ Ernest Blevins

Compassion means that if I see my friend and my enemy in equal need, I shall help both equally. Justice demands that we seek and find the stranger, the broken, the prisoner and comfort them and offer them our help. Here lies the holy compassion of God.
~ Mechtild of Magdeburg

The value of compassion cannot be overemphasized. Anyone can criticize. It takes a true believer to be compassionate. No greater burden can be borne by an individual than to know no one cares or understands.
~ Arthur H. Stainback

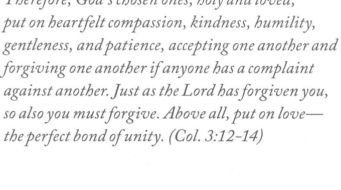

*Therefore, God's chosen ones, holy and loved,
put on heartfelt compassion, kindness, humility,
gentleness, and patience, accepting one another and
forgiving one another if anyone has a complaint
against another. Just as the Lord has forgiven you,
so also you must forgive. Above all, put on love—
the perfect bond of unity. (Col. 3:12–14)*

Prayer:

Father, You have such unconditional love and compassion for us that we can scarcely take it in. Help us to have this kind of love for others, no matter what may be their skin color, country of origin, or belief system. Help us to see each other as Your children no matter where we are. Amen.

Heart Strings

Lofty Thoughts and Attitudes

Set your minds on what is above, not on what is on the earth. (Col. 3:2)

Love just naturally causes you to think better thoughts. It lifts you up and raises your heartbeat. Raising your heartbeat gives you more energy and before you know it, the whole world looks like a better place. The wonderful part of it all is this. It's all about your thoughts. Your thoughts shape your attitude.

I've heard it said that we should watch out for our "stinkin' thinkin'." Perhaps along with that idea, we should watch out for our "shrinking thinking." How often do our thoughts set limits, criticizing our hopes and dreams and causing our hearts to build walls and borders to protect us from failure or loss.

When you set your mind on the earth, you'll get bogged down to the lowest possible level, shrinking with every step, losing sight of heaven. When you

65

set your mind on heaven, you'll open up your possibilities on every level and you'll get earth thrown in. Lofty thoughts open doors.

Change your thoughts
and you change your world.
~ Norman Vincent Peale

The LORD of Hosts says this:
"Think carefully about your ways." (Hag. 1:7)

The greatest gift
is a portion of thyself.
~ Ralph Waldo Emerson

We cannot help conforming
ourselves to what we love.
~ Francis of Sales

Prayer:
Lord, I know that my attitude about anything makes all the difference. I know that when I focus on troubles and trials, that my light becomes dim with worry and regret. Help me to set my mind on You and on the things above, so that I can meet the world with joy. Amen.

Heart Strings

Love: One of the Essentials of Life

"I give you a new commandment: Love one another. Just as I have loved you, you must also love one another. By this all people will know that you are My disciples, if you have love for one another." (John 13:34–35)

If we think about those things we might consider to be the opposites of love, things like: hate, fear, apathy, evil, gossip, cruelty, and others, it becomes clear that life without love is empty and dark. Those without love become fearful and lonely. They resist the light of love.

Therefore, love is essential to our good health and our well-being. It is important to our success as human beings and in the work we do. There simply is no real living without love.

If we could truly grasp the importance of love in our lives, we would be more driven to protect it, to nurture it when it begins to show itself, and to hold it close when it comes to us. Whatever else you do today, hold love close to you and honor it with your whole heart.

The value of life lies not in the length of days, but in the use we make of them.
~ Michel de Montaigne

There is no principle of the heart that is more acceptable to God than a universal, ardent love for all mankind, which seeks and prays for their happiness.
~ William Law

There are three material things essential to life. These are pure air, water, and earth. There are three immaterial things essential to life. These are admiration, hope, and love.

ADMIRATION—the power of discerning and taking delight in what is beautiful in visible form and lovely in human character and, necessarily, striving to produce what is beautiful in form and to become what is lovely in character.

HOPE—the recognition, by true foresight, of better things to be reached hereafter, whether by ourselves or others necessarily issuing in the straight-forward and undisappointable effort to advance, according to our proper power, the gaining of them.

LOVE—both of family and neighbor, faithful and satisfying.

~ John Ruskin

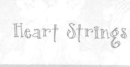

ENOUGH OF LOVE!

What if love
Walked out the door,
Disappeared,
Was no more?
What would your heart do?
What if love
Just said good—bye,
Just can't stay,
Gotta fly!
And left you feeling blue?

What if love
Had had enough,
Just don't need
This crazy stuff
Where would you be then?

Love Is Calling

Well, love may seem
  a little short
May withdraw its main
  support,
May even seem to pass you by,
But it's not gone, and here is why.

Love is God's true m.o.,
It's the one place you can go,
Anytime you're feeling low
And His Word will tell you so.
The Source of love
Is always strong,
He won't opt out
Or steer you
  wrong.

He won't leave you
All alone,
Won't give up
On joys you've known.

'Cause you're His child
For always and ever,
His heart's desire,
From now, and forever.

So His love holds you
When times are tough,
And in His grace,
Love IS enough!
~Karen Moore

Prayer:
Thank You, Lord, for making love the focus of all Your efforts, all Your work here on Earth. Thank You for sharing Your heart and Your spirit with us so that we can learn to give and to receive real love. Help us to share love with others who feel alone and to come to You when we need more love for ourselves. We know You have enough love to go around to all Your children everywhere. Amen.

About that "Love Your Neighbor" Thing . . .

*Just as you want others to do for you,
do the same for them. (Luke 6:31)*

Some people aren't very clear about that "love your neighbor" thing. They aren't sure who the neighbors are. Sure, they may have people next door, or in the mobile home park, or at the apartment complex, but they don't know them. Of course, the people you live around and the ones you work with, by definition are your most immediate neighbors. They're the people you rely on even if you don't know each other well. They're the people nearby so you want to treat them well. Be neighborly!

Whoever you choose to call a "neighbor" doesn't matter nearly as much as how you treat them. Jesus reminded us to treat others the way we want to be treated, the Golden Rule.

77

It used to be a little easier for neighbors to help each other and watch out for each other. Now, it's more difficult because the world is shrinking and your neighbors who seek your help may come through the Internet or your TV screen.

Clearly, no one can take care of the whole world, but you can still be neighborly and share a little love each time you pray for those in need, or lend a hand to someone who can't pay you back, or just offer a kind word or smile. When you do, you pass on the love and the blessing. That's being a good neighbor to everyone.

Do not waste time bothering
about whether you love your neighbor;
act as if you did . . .
When you are behaving
as if you love someone,
you will presently come to love him.
~ C. S. Lewis

Charity begins at home,
and justice begins next door.
~ Charles Dickens

The love of God is the first
and great commandment.
But love of our neighbor
is the means by which we obey it.
Since we cannot see God directly,
God allows us to catch sight
of Him through our neighbor.
By loving our neighbor
we purge our eyes to see God.
So love your neighbor and
you will discover that in doing so
you come to know God.
~ St. Augustine

There is no principle
of the heart
that is more acceptable
to God than a universal,
ardent love for all mankind,
which seeks and prays for
their happiness.
~William Law

Prayer:

Thank You for good neighbors.
Thank You that You have put us
near those who can share the joys
of life and comfort us in sorrow.
Help us to treat each other with
grace and mercy as You treat us.
Amen.

Love In Action

And whatever you do, in word or in deed,
do everything in the name of the Lord Jesus,
giving thanks to God the Father through Him.
(Col. 3:17)

Have you ever had someone give you a gift unexpectedly? Perhaps they were shopping and they saw something that reminded them so much of you, they felt compelled to buy it, or they simply knew how much you would enjoy it. Love does that! Love finds a way to please others by doing little things that bring joy.

Sometimes we show love for others by being able to say just the right thing, offer a kind word of encouragement, or share a good laugh. Sometimes we simply share a conversation that brought us closer together and reminded us of how much we mean to each other. Our hearts are grateful for moments of kind words or sweet gifts.

As we look out at the world today, seek those sweet moments when you might just share a little unexpected "love" with someone, offering them the gift of your encouragement, your kind words, or even a smile. Love is always a verb and you can put it into action any time!

Love cannot be practiced right
unless we first exercise it the moment
God gives the opportunity.
~ John Wesley

*Every devotion must give way to a work
of love to the spiritual and to the
physical man. For even should one rise
in prayer higher than Peter or Paul,
and hear that a poor man needed a drink
of water, he would have to cease from the
devotional exercise, sweet though
it were, and do the deed of love.*
~ John of Ruysbroeck

How far that little candle
Throws his beams!
So shines a good deed
In a weary world.
~William Shakespeare

A kind heart is a fountain
of gladness, making everything in its
vicinity freshen into smiles.
~ Washington Irving

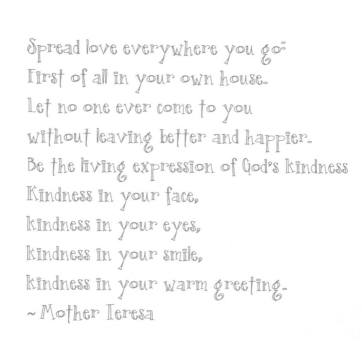

Spread love everywhere you go:
First of all in your own house.
Let no one ever come to you
without leaving better and happier.
Be the living expression of God's kindness
Kindness in your face,
kindness in your eyes,
kindness in your smile,
kindness in your warm greeting.
~ Mother Teresa

Prayer:
Father, You have been so kind to us. You have given us all we need to be happy in this world. Help us to be loving and kind and willing to share Your love with others. Amen.

Heart Strings

Of Hearts and Flowers

A good man produces good out of the good storeroom of his heart. (Luke 6:45)

You've probably done a lot of good deeds in your life. Isn't it fun to imagine your heart as a kind of storeroom, a space where you can stockpile bits of joy and kindness that you'll share with others? This truly makes your heart a treasure chest of opportunity.

Since we know that our actions are primarily heart matters, then it's important to always plant seeds of love. It is those very seeds that become the flowers of beautiful words said just at the right time, or blossoms of hope that encourage the path of someone who feels lost and alone. You have a storehouse of hearts and flowers to share and God is gracious enough to bring you opportunities to keep it full and growing.

As you consider each person near you who means the world to you, who needs some extra hearts and flowers today, walk through your storehouse of grace and mercy and pick the most beautiful joys to share. It will surely do your heart good!

Serve with a good attitude, as to the Lord and not to men. (Eph. 6:7)

A Christian should always remember that the value of his good works is not based on their number and excellence, but on the love of God which prompts him to do these things.
~ John of the Cross

Did it ever strike you that goodness is not merely a beautiful thing, but by far the most beautiful thing in the whole world? So that nothing is to be compared for value with goodness that riches, honor, power, pleasure, learning, the whole world and all in it, are not worth having in comparison with being good and the utterly best thing for a man or woman is to be good, even though they were never rewarded for it. ~ Charles Kingsley

*We have a call to do good, as often as
we have the power and the occasion.*
~ William Penn

Prayer:
Lord, we can hardly imagine the love You have for us and the goodness of Your spirit toward all of Your creation. Help us to share what we have and who we are in You in every way that brings joy to others. Amen.

A Look at Shining Armor

*Put on the full armor of God. . . . Stand, therefore,
with truth like a belt around your waist, righteousness
like armor on your chest, and your feet sandaled with
readiness for the gospel of peace. In every situation
take the shield of faith, and with it you will be able to
extinguish the flaming arrows of the evil one. Take
the helmet of salvation, and the sword of the Spirit,
which is God's word. (Eph. 6:11, 14–17)*

You may have found your knight in shining armor
or your favorite lady, or you may still be searching
for the love of your life, but either way, the search for
love has captured our hearts and imaginations
since Adam and Eve were in the garden.
Fortunately, they truly were made for each other.
The rest of us have had to discover God's choice
for us by a lot of trial and error, or a bit of chance
and grace.

Whatever we do to find a true life partner, it all takes a little preparation and it's not a bad idea to suit up for the search. After all, putting on the armor of God means we'll be decked out in ways that we can attract the best kind of love.

Imagine finding someone who was actually willing to tell you the truth about themselves. Right from the start, they were honest and full of integrity. They had a zest for life and an almost child-like innocence that captured your heart and your attention. Add to that the feeling of total comfort and peace you experience each time you're standing in their presence, almost like you're at home.

With a little faith and love, this person may well be the one you've been seeking, your true knight in shining armor. Keep your heart open and faith strong. Love always finds a way.

Life is to be fortified by many friendships. To love and to be loved is the greatest happiness of existence.
~ Sydney Smith

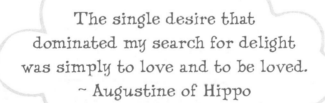

The single desire that dominated my search for delight was simply to love and to be loved.
~ Augustine of Hippo

To love another person is to see the face of God.
~Victor Hugo

Joy is love exalted, peace is
love in repose, long-suffering is
love enduring, gentleness is love
in society, goodness is love in
action, faith is love on the
battlefield meekness is love in
school, and temperance is love
in training.
~D. L. Moody

Prayer:
Lord, You have given us all we need to seek love and protect it. Help us to be willing to wear the full armor of Your spirit so that when we find love we may give it the best of all we have. Help us to shine from within according to Your will and purpose in all our relationships. Amen.

Wishing You Love and Laughter

And we have come to know and to believe the love that God has for us. God is love, and the one who remains in love remains in God, and God remains in him. (1 John 4:16)

It has been said that we cannot truly love anyone with whom we can't laugh. Surely we all recognize how valuable a good laugh shared with friends can be and it's so much more when we share laughter with those we love.

When you laugh, you share your spirit and sense of joy. You share your vulnerability in a way that's different than sharing tears. You share a side of yourself that is often more at peace.

Any relationship we have with others has ups and downs, moments of connection and moments of division. Laughter can be healing and helpful in bringing you back together and helping you forgive each other too.

Whenever you have a chance to see things on the lighter side, you can often bring things to the brighter side. Inject your relationships with more reasons to laugh. It's a sure way to watch love grow and laughter is good for the soul.

Laughter is the shortest distance
between two people.
~ Victor Borge

Of all the things God created, I am often
most grateful He created laughter.
~ Charles Swindoll

A good laugh is sunshine in a house.
~ William Makepeace Thackeray

Laughter can relieve tension,
soothe the pain of disappointment, and
strengthen the spirit for the formidable
tasks that always lie ahead.
~ Dwight D. Eisenhower

HAPPILY EVER AFTER!

For any love relationship
To grow happily ever after,
There must be daily doses
Of outrageous love and laughter.
~Karen Moore

Prayer:
Lord, we thank You for giving each of us a sense of humor. Help us to look for the sunny side of our relationships and share our love with others with warmth and laughter. Amen.

Oh, My Perfect Love!

There is no fear in love; instead, perfect love drives out fear, because fear involves punishment. So the one who fears has not reached perfection in love. We love because He first loved us. (1 John 4:18–19)

We may always fall short of finding perfect love, though we can hope for "perfect for me" love and be pretty satisfied with that. Perfect love hardly seems attainable, somewhat in the same category as winning the Nobel Prize or the Lottery. It's a Cinderella fantasy that leaves us wondering.

If we consider the statement, "There is no fear in love" then we may have to take a good hard look at our relationships. Have we ever had a love relationship that did not come with assorted fears and worries? Chances are slim.

If we think about the relationship of Jesus with His heavenly Father, or with His friends on earth, one thing we never saw from him was fear. He existed in love. He knew perfect love.

On occasion, we get a glimpse of perfect love, moments when no fears exist and everything comes together in total joy. Imagine what it will be like when we are once and forever bound by His perfect love.

Perfection stands in a man offering all his heart wholly to God, not seeking himself or his own will, either in great things or in small, in time or in eternity, but abiding always unchanged and always yielding to God equal thanks for things pleasing and displeasing, weighing them all in one same balance, as in His love.
~ Thomas à Kempis

No saint on earth can be fully perfect and pure.
~ Martin Luther

Prayer:
Lord, there can be no perfect love but Yours. We thank You for loving us just as we are and raising us up to be more than we could ever be alone. We thank You and give You praise. Amen.

Heart Strings

Take My Hand!

Only carefully obey the command and instruction that Moses the LORD's servant gave you: to love the LORD your God, walk in all His ways, keep His commands, remain faithful to Him, and serve Him with all your heart and all your soul. (Josh. 22:5)

Do you remember the feeling you had the first time someone you really liked held your hand? That simple connection somehow made you feel more special, more in tune with each other. Holding hands meant that you were there for each other and it made your heart glow a little.

People you love still need your gentle touch, a chance to hold your hand or walk beside you. They need that one on one moment when there's no one else as important as they are to you.

The world is big, and sometimes we can feel lost in it. Having a gentle hand to hold can make all the difference about how your heart copes with what life brings your way.

Whenever you have an opportunity, take the hand of the person you love and remind them how happy you are to be walking through life with them, how much it means to you to be so sweetly connected, heart to heart and hand to hand.

Just as God always walks closely by your side, ready at a moment's notice to help you along or bring you comfort, walk with those you love in the same way. Holding hands is simply a beautiful message of love.

We do not walk to God with the feet of our body, nor would wings, if we had them, carry us to Him, but we go to Him, by the affections of our soul.
~ Augustine of Hippo

Little things console us because little things afflict us.
~ Pascal

If I alone might have all the solace and comfort of this world, and might use the delights of this world according to my own desire and without sin, it is certain that they would not long endure. And so, my soul cannot be fully comforted or perfectly refreshed, except in God alone, who is the Comforter of the poor in spirit and the Embracer of the humble and the low in heart.

~ Thomas à Kempis

No one may forsake his neighbor when he is in trouble. Everybody is under obligation to help and support his neighbor as he would himself like to be helped.

~ Martin Luther

True happiness . . . arises, in the first place, from the enjoyment of one's self, and, in the next, from friendship and conversation of a few selected companions.

~ Joseph Addison

109

WALKING HAND IN HAND

It was just a simple gesture,
Certainly, not planned;
A natural kind of feeling
As we walked hand in hand.

You closed your fingers over mine,
And drew my heart to You,
We walked on in joy and love
As good friends often do.
There's something sweet and special
That makes the heart feel light
When you're walking hand in hand
       And the whole world
         feels just right.
        ~Karen Moore

Prayer:
Lord, there's something very special about knowing You walk the way with us all the time, heart to heart and hand to hand. Thank You for choosing to be near us any time at all. Help us to walk more intentionally with You and more closely with each other. Amen.

Heart Strings

Sweet Morsels... those Kind Words!

*Your speech should always be gracious, seasoned
with salt, so that you know how you should answer
each person. (Col. 4:6)*

If you received a chocolate candy kiss for every kind
word you spoke in any given day, would you have a
huge bowl full by the day's end, or would you find just a
morsel or two? The sweetness of a kind word at just the
right moment cannot be measured, but it will always
be treasured.

Nothing breaks the heart and the spirit more than
when you feel misunderstood, or verbally abused, or
judged and accused by people who don't walk in your
shoes. The world can be a harsh
place and so the best opportunity
to be refreshed and renewed often
comes from the sanctuary of your
own home, the place where they love
you unconditionally.

At least, that's the goal, to learn to love the people closest to you with your whole heart, without restraint or conditions. When you do, you'll always know just the right thing to say, or just when to stay quiet. You'll know how to offer comfort and strength. You'll be the sweet little morsel of a chocolate kiss, just in the nick of time. You can never get enough of kind words. Try it and see!

Just because an animal is large,
it doesn't mean he doesn't want kindness,
however big Tigger seems to be, remember that
he wants as much kindness as Roo.
~ *Winnie the Pooh*, by A. A. Milne

Keep your words soft and sweet.
You never know when
you're going to have to eat them.
~ Unknown Author

Kind words can be short and easy to
speak but their echoes are truly endless.
~ Mother Teresa

Prayer:

Father, all of us need to feel the kindness of others. We need to feel valued and loved and we need to share our hearts. Help us to always be mindful of what we speak and to offer each other the sweet taste of joy through our words. In Jesus' name we pray. Amen.

Taking Time for Love

There is an occasion for everything, and a time for every activity under heaven . . . a time to love and a time to hate; a time for war and a time for peace. (Eccles. 3:1, 8)

Perhaps you don't really stop to consider whether or not you "take time for love" but it might be worth the effort. After all, your willingness to interact with those around you in loving ways speaks volumes about how you value them. You have to be conscious of love and feed and nurture it for it to grow.

So, how can you take time for love? Here are a few possibilities:

- You can plan something special for someone you love.
- You can engage in warm conversation.
- You can create a card.
- You can purchase a simple gift.

- You can go the extra mile to treat them well.
- You can share your heart.
- You can go for a walk, hand in hand.
- You can pray together.
- You can bake a cake.
- You can notice something about them and pay a compliment.
- You can teach them something you enjoy doing.
- You can admire something they've created.
- You can offer to lend a hand.
- You can serve them by doing small errands or favors without having been asked . . . wash their car, or do the laundry.
- You can smile and let them know you're fully present for them.
- You can dance around the kitchen.

Whatever you do, know that you're building sweet memories. There's nothing quite as wonderful as creating a new scrapbook of precious moments you've shared together. Whenever you embrace love, the rewards are unending.

Now the goal of our instruction is love that comes from a pure heart, a good conscience, and a sincere faith. (1 Tim. 1:5)

Take more time for love today.

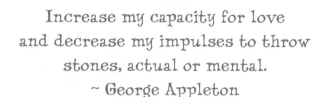

Increase my capacity for love
and decrease my impulses to throw
stones, actual or mental.
~ George Appleton

*You will find, as you look back upon your
life, that the moments when you really
lived are the moments when you have
done things in the spirit of love.*
~ Henry Drummond

This is the miracle that happens every
time to those who really love, the more
they give, the more they possess.
~ Rainer Maria Rilke

*Accustom yourself
continually to make many
arts of love, for they re-
kindle and melt the soul.*
~ Teresa of Avila

NO TIME FOR LOVE

I woke up in the morning,
Love called out to me,
I said, "I don't have time
 just now,
You'll have to let me be."

I stopped at lunch to get a bite
And love was there again,
"Come with me," it whispered,
"You can be my friend."

"Too busy now," I answered,
"Love will have to wait,"
"Don't wait too long," love
called again,
"For it might be too late."

I stopped then to consider
Perhaps love could be right,
So then and there I changed my plans
And kept love in my sight.

I shared love with my family,
I shared my heart each day,
And ever since I've smiled
That love showed me the way!
~Karen Moore

Prayer:
Lord, help us to not neglect our opportunities to show love and to share love with those who are dear to us. Help us to love others as ourselves and to discover through others what it means to love You. Help us always to be willing to take time for love in every possible way. Amen.

Heart Strings

Love Grows through the Years!

But grow in the grace and knowledge of our Lord and Savior Jesus Christ. To Him be the glory both now and to the day of eternity. (2 Pet. 3:18)

Love sustained over time has a beauty all its own. It is a portrait of all that has built its foundation. Those who are blessed with years have a history together that took two individuals and created one strong union. Love moved from dreams to memories, from what might be to what is, from all that we hope for to all that we know.

As you look at the person or even the people in your life who have sheltered and nurtured you, or prayed for you for years, or who have simply encouraged you to become all that you are, give thanks for them. Ask God to grant them endless grace and mercy for the unselfish and unconditional love they have given you.

125

Whether long term love is between two people, or shared by members of the same family, or even enduring friendships, it is a thing to be prized. Look at those you've loved over the years, who have helped you grow, and praise God for the gift they have been to you. It's such a blessing to have a history of love that has grown over the years.

Grow old along with me!
The best is yet to be.
The last of life, for which the first
   was made
Our times are in his hand
Who said, "A whole I planned,
Youth shows but half trust God:
   see all,
Nor be afraid."
~Robert Browning

He is only advancing in life, whose heart is getting softer, his blood warmer, his brain quicker, and his spirit entering into living peace.
~ John Ruskin

There is within every soul
a thirst for happiness and meaning.
~ Thomas Aquinas

God intended marriage for the mutual society, help and comfort that the one ought to have of the other both in prosperity and adversity.
~ Book of Common Prayer

Be the mate
God designed you to be.
~ Anthony T. Evans

127

There is no more lovely, friendly or charming relationship, communion or company, than a good marriage.
~ Martin Luther

Lord, when we are wrong, make us willing to change. And when we are right, make us easy to live with.
~ Peter Marshall

People are just about as happy as they make up their minds to be.
~ Abraham Lincoln

Those who love deeply never grow old;
they may die of old age,
but they die young.
~Sir Arthur Wing Pinero

Prayer:
Lord, thank You for the kind of relationships that are sustained over time. Thank You for the people who love and protect us, keep us healthy, and accept us just as we are. Bless all Your people who create warm and enduring relationships and grow together through the years. Amen.

Heart Strings

Love Letters

You yourselves are our letter, written on our hearts, recognized and read by everyone. It is clear that you are Christ's letter, produced by us, not written with ink but with the Spirit of the living God—not on stone tablets but on tablets that are hearts of flesh. (2 Cor. 3:2–3)

Do you remember the last time you received a love letter? Perhaps it was written on beautiful stationery with little flourishes like flowers and hearts. Perhaps it was scented with a delightful fragrance that caused your heart to skip a beat. Maybe it had a beautiful poem attached. Whatever form it may have taken, it was a pure delight to your soul.

Love letters are getting to be a thing of the past, something that may have been popular in the Victorian Age or in the days before the Internet and e-mails. In any case, there's nothing quite as touching as sending and receiving a real letter of love.

131

The Bible has been called a love letter from God to His people. It contains all that He would have us know about His plans for us and His love for us. It reminds us that He is always with us and that He watches over us all the days of our lives. It's God's way of romancing us so that our desire for Him becomes stronger all the time.

If you haven't done it in a long time, maybe this is a good time for you to find some lovely stationery, a good thesaurus if you need help with the words, and share your heart with someone you love. It will be a lasting keepsake, one that your loved one will read over and over again. Perhaps that is the hope God had when He inspired the biblical writers as well.

Put your heart into every line.

Everyone reveals his own soul in his letters. In every other form of composition it is possible to discern the writer's character, but in none so clearly as the epistolary.
~ Demetrius

The most original authors are not so because they advance what is new, but because they put what they have to say as if it had never been said before. ~ Goethe

So let us love, dear Love,
   like as we ought.
Love is the lesson
   which the Lord us taught.
~Edmund Spenser

Prayer:

Lord, thank You for Your love letter to us. We know that the Bible was inspired by Your hand so that we might read it over and over again and come to know and love You more. Help us be willing to write letters of love to people who bring great joy to our lives. Help us to never step aside from a chance to express our love more fully to the people around us. In Jesus' name we pray. Amen.

The Many Kinds of Love

Love does no wrong to a neighbor. Love, therefore, is the fulfillment of the law. (Rom. 13:10)

If there's any word in the English language that gets bandied about to the place of almost losing its meaning, it's the word *love*. Love is an expression of passion, both for another person and your favorite football team or college. It's what we say when we have favorite foods or favorite colors. "I love pizza," or "I love all things red."

We love, love! So, how do we make sure that we express love, that deeper heartfelt kind, in the ways that others can recognize it from us? How can we make our feelings of love stand apart from the hundreds of material or physical things we love? Let's put the meaning back in the word *love*.

The point here is not to say that there's anything wrong with the various aspects and objects of love. What we want though is to recognize the difference in things we attribute love to, and the things we commit to love. We commit to love our spouse or our children. We commit to love God. We commit to love our neighbors as ourselves and that means we need to know a whole lot about what it means to love ourselves.

This is a new day, a new chance for you to define what you mean each time you use the word *love*. You may surprise yourself as you consider it. You may find that you do indeed love everything around you. Commit to love wherever you find it.

Love one another in truth and purity,
as children, impulsively, uncalculatingly.
~ Edward Wilson

Charity means love.
It is called Agape in the
New Testament to distinguish
it from Eros (sexual love),
Storge (family affection)
and Philia (friendship).
So there are four kinds of love,
all good in their proper place,
but Agape is the best because
it is the kind of love God has for us
and is good in all circumstances.
~ C. S. Lewis

Love of God is the root,
love of our neighbor the fruit
of the Tree of Life.
Neither can exist without
the other, but the one is cause
and the other effect.
~ William Temple

THE MOSAIC OF LOVE

I picked a bright red flower,
A rose upon the vine,
And put it in a scrapbook,
So I could call it mine.

I stood before the preacher,
In a gown of lace and white,
And placed a ring upon your hand
With love and sweet delight.

Love Is Calling

I hugged my baby daughter,
And took her photo too,
So I could catch the memory
Of love so sweet and new.

I traveled over land and sea,
To places far from home,
And cherished the adventures
And the chance I had to roam.

I stopped to say a prayer to God,
Thankful for each part,
Of Mosaics in the picture—
Of the love from His great heart.
~Karen Moore

*It is possible to love your friends,
your competitors, and even your
enemies. It is hard, bitterly hard,
but there is a long distance between
hard and impossible.
~ Herbert Webb*

Agape (love) means understanding,
redeeming good will for all persons.
It is an overflowing love which is purely
spontaneous, unmotivated, groundless,
and creative. It is not set in motion by
any quality or function of its object.
It is the love of God operating
in the human heart.
~ Martin Luther King Jr.

Prayer:
Lord, You have blessed us with
so many ways to discover what it
means to love. We can love each
other, we can love the beauty of
this planet, and we can love life in
its richness and glory, all because
of You. Thank You, for loving us so
much! Amen.

Heart Strings

Love Is the Verb of Virtue

For this very reason, make every effort to supplement your faith with goodness, goodness with knowledge, knowledge with self-control, self-control with endurance, endurance with godliness, godliness with brotherly affection, and brotherly affection with love. (2 Pet. 1:5-7)

Since we know love is a verb of action, it stands to reason that love comes with a requirement. The requirement is simply this. Each day we must strive to love more. We must seek to be more loving tomorrow than we were able to be today. Why? Because God is love and all things that emanate from love are rewarded with the joy of having even more love in your life.

Love that is borne of brotherly affection has compassion on others. It is empathetic when tragedy befalls a neighbor or when tears spring from the eyes of a friend. It prompts us to desire to do more for each other and that desire brings us closer to God. When we're closer to God we know that we can endure all things, we can trust with our whole heart that God will see us through. We are designed with the ability to be virtuous people. We are created in the image of the One who loves us more than we can imagine and who rejoices each time we learn to love others more.

It's a new day! It's your chance to show others the great love stored in your heart, ready to be given to those who are ready to receive it. Act in love today.

Only through love
can we attain communion with God.
~Albert Schweitzer

*Just as bitterness produces
more bitterness in others,
so love begets love.*
~ Alan Loy McGinnis

Jesus said love one another.
He didn't say love the whole world.
~ Mother Teresa

*The day will come when, after
harvesting space, the winds, the tides,
and gravitation, we shall harness for God
the energies of love. And on that day, for
the second time in the history of the
world, we shall have discovered fire.*
~ Pierre Teilhard de Chardin

If love is the soul of the Christian
experience, it must be at the heart
of every other Christian virtue.
Thus, for example,
justice without love is legalism,
faith without love is ideology,
hope without love is self—centeredness,
forgiveness without love is self—abasement,
fortitude without love is recklessness,
generosity without love is extravagance,
care without love is mere duty,
fidelity without love is servitude.
Every virtue is an expression of love.
No virtue is really
a virtue unless it
is permeated, or
informed, by love.
~ Richard P. McBrien

*The greatest virtues
are those which are most
useful to other persons.*
~ Aristotle

I pronounce it as certain
that there was never a truly
great man that was not at
the same time truly virtuous.
~ Benjamin Franklin

*Virtue dwells not in the tongue,
but in the heart.*
~ Thomas Fuller

Do your utmost
to guard your heart,
for out of it comes life.
~ Walter Hilton

Heart Strings

If your heart were sincere and upright,
every creature would be unto you
a looking-glass of life and a
book of holy doctrine.
~ Thomas à Kempis

The service we render to
others is really the rent we pay
for our room on this earth.
~ Unknown Author

Our true worth does not consist in
what human beings think of us.
What we really are is what
God knows us to be.
~ John Berchmans

Prayer:
Lord, You know who we are and what virtues and what faults exist within us. Open our hearts to those around us that we may love them in some small way as much as You do. Let us always act in love to one another. Amen.

Falling in Love . . . Again!

Mighty waters cannot extinguish love;
rivers cannot sweep it away. (Song of Songs 8:7)

Nothing tugs at your heartstrings like falling in love. Sometimes you fall hard and fast. Sometimes you hardly notice that it happened until the moment when you call it by name.

Nothing stirs the heart like love. Nothing fascinates the spirit, opening the mind to possibilities never before imagined like love. However it happens, whenever it happens, count it all for joy.

The world may try to convince you to get along without love, to even detach from love so that you can get your work done and accomplish your goals. It may even deceive you into thinking you're unworthy of love. Nothing could be further from the truth.

As a child of God, you are already unconditionally loved. You are already the apple of God's eye. Take a moment to absorb that thought and sit with it. Allow yourself to feel God's love for you.

That feeling of love is the one you pass on to others. When you do, you can fall in love again and again. You may fall in love with the same person many times in your relationship. Love changes and grows.

You may fall in love with a new person, or you may fall in love with the God of your heart over and over again.

Nothing renews and refreshes your spirit like love, no matter how many times you fall.

Love does not die easily. It is a living thing. It thrives in the face of all life's hazards, save one—neglect.
~ James D. Bryden

Real love is a force more formidable than any other. It is invisible—it cannot be seen or measured, yet it is powerful enough to transform you in a moment, and offer you more joy than any material possession could.
~ Barbara DeAngelis

We cannot help conforming ourselves to what we love. ~ Francis de Sales

In labors of love, every day is payday.
~ Gaines Brewster

Prayer:
Lord, because You loved us first,
we have the privilege and the joy
of loving others. We learn to fall
for You in new ways continually.
We stand in awe at Your creation
and our hearts melt. We look on
the scars of Your son and we are
awed by what He has done for us.
You have provided ways for us to
fall in love with each new dawn.
Thank You for loving us so much.
Amen.

Heart Strings

Sugar & Spice, and Everything Nice!

You have heard that it was said, Love your neighbor and hate your enemy. But I tell you, love your enemies and pray for those who persecute you, so that you may be sons of your Father in heaven. For He causes His sun to rise on the evil and the good, and sends rain on the righteous and the unrighteous. For if you love those who love you, what reward will you have? (Matt. 5:43–46)

One of the aspects of being a loving person that may cause us to want to ignore its truth is that of loving those who seem unlovable to us. Perhaps it's a worthy exercise to pause for a moment and see if there's anyone or anything that pops into your mind with the classification of "enemy."

You might think that you have no enemies, but on closer inspection realize that you are a bit biased about certain organizations or types of people. You may find a neighbor who just sets off your alarms in ways that don't make you happy. What should you do?

As we contemplate our heartstrings, it brings God joy to have us recognize the limitations on our willingness to love. It's not that we're not capable, but we've set our minds in a direction to not allow love in.

Imagine being a truly loving person. Imagine opening your heart to your neighbors in ways you've never embraced before. Perhaps in that alone you'll experience a new reward. Toss in the sugar and spice whenever you can!

The desire of power in excess caused the angels to fall; the desire of knowledge in excess caused man to fall; but in love there is no excess, neither can angel or man come in danger by it.
~ Francis Bacon

He alone loves the Creator
perfectly who manifests
a pure love for his neighbor.
~ Venerable Bede

We are too ready to retaliate
rather than to forgive
or to gain by love and information.
Let us, then, try what love will do
for if men do once see we love them,
we should find they would not harm us.
~William Penn

159

Love must be learned
again and again . . .
Hate needs no instruction,
but waits only to be provoked.
~ Katherine Anne Porter

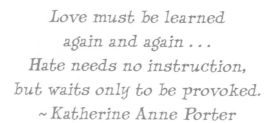

The one who will be found
in trial capable of great acts of love,
is ever the one who is doing
considerate small ones.
~ F. W. Robertson

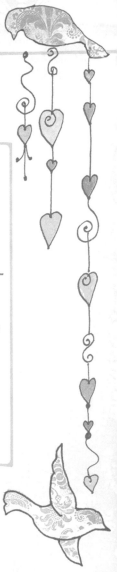

Prayer:
Lord, You have worked within us to broaden our scope and understanding of what it means to love. You have commanded us and challenged us to love one another. Help us in all ways and in all that we do to show that love to each person we meet without judgment or hidden agendas. Help us to truly love our neighbors. Amen.

The Give and Take of Love

Each person should do as he has decided in his heart—not reluctantly or out of necessity, for God loves a cheerful giver. And God is able to make every grace overflow to you, so that in every way, always having everything you need, you may excel in every good work. (2 Cor. 9:7–8)

By now you've figured out that the best kind of love is one where you have a sense of joyful giving. In the process of giving, you discover that you receive more than you ever dreamed possible. God is a Giver. He's taught us that there's far more joy in a giving heart than in one that seeks always to benefit from anything it may do.

The wonderful thing about being a giver is that giving is in itself a gift that keeps perpetuating.

Like love, the more you learn to give, the more you can get, because God's grace overflows in everything around you, giving back to you in ways that mere human relationships can never quite accomplish.

The give and take of any relationship is what helps it thrive, helps it mature and become sustainable. It's in both giving and receiving that you recognize what love really is and what happiness that kind of love generates. All of us need to be able to give to someone or to something that we have a passion for because if we don't, our light gets diminished and our capacity for love hides itself away.

On the other hand, there's no greater result of love than knowing someone genuinely cares about you and enjoys helping to create a sense of peace and joy in your life. In love, we're humbled by the things we receive.

Go ahead, give a little. Open your heart to receive as well and love will bless you every day of your life.

We make a living by what we get.
We make a life by what we give.
~ Winston Churchill

A cheerful giver does not
count the cost of what he gives.
His heart is set on pleasing and
cheering him to whom
the gift is given.
~ Julian of Norwich

Giving is the secret
of a healthy life.
Not necessarily money,
but whatever a man has of
encouragement and sympathy
and understanding.
~ John D. Rockefeller Jr.

We never know how much one loves till we know how much he is willing to endure and suffer for us and it is the suffering element that measures love. The characters that are great must, of necessity, be characters that shall be willing, patient and strong to endure for others. To hold our nature in the willing service of another is the divine idea of manhood, of the human character.
~ Henry Ward Beecher

Charity is twice blessed—
it blesses the one who gives
and the one who receives.
~ Author Unknown

Give strength,
Give thought,
Give deeds,
Give wealth
Give love,
Give tears,
And give thyself.
Give, give, be always giving.
Who gives not
Is not living
The more you give,
The more you live.
~Author Unknown

*Loving one another with the charity of
Christ, let the love you have in your
hearts be shown outwardly in your deeds
so that compelled by such an example,
you may also grow in the love of God
and charity for one another.*
~ Clare of Assisi (adapted)

Being happy with God now means:
    Loving as he loves,
    Helping as he helps,
    Giving as he gives,
    Serving as he serves,
    Rescuing as he rescues,
    Being with him twenty-four hours,
    Touching him in his distressing disguise.
    ~Mother Teresa

Prayer:

Lord, thank you for your divine examples of what it means to give and to receive love. Help us to be aware of those around us and offer to them a portion of love that will sustain them. Help our hearts to be open to ways we can be generous givers to all those we love. In Jesus' name. Amen.

169

Contented, Cozy Love

I don't say this out of need, for I have learned to be content in whatever circumstances I am. I know both how to have a little, and I know how to have a lot. In any and all circumstances I have learned the secret of being content—whether well fed or hungry, whether in abundance or in need. I am able to do all things through Him who strengthens me. (Phil. 4:11–13)

One of the delightful results of love is that it often helps us to feel more content with life. We look at the person or the people who surround us with love and feel more connected to work, play, and the environment. It feels like all is well with the world.

When God noticed that Adam was lonely as he wandered around in the beautiful garden, surrounded by all manner of fascinating creatures and feasts for the eyes, He stopped what He was doing. He immediately realized how important relationships are to the human spirit.

He created a suitable being for Adam so that someone would be near to experience all that life had to offer.

Love, any form of love that we have with those around us, brings us that warmth and connection, that joyous awareness that we're not alone in the world.

As you look at those you love today, bless them. Thank them for what they do to contribute a sense of well-being to your life. Thank them for helping you live in contentment no matter what your circumstances may be. May God's peace be with you always.

Next to faith, this is the highest art—
to be content with the calling in which God
has placed you. I have not learned it yet.
~ Martin Luther

Everything that God has effected has been
perfected in Love, Humility and Peace.
Human beings, therefore, should esteem
Love, embrace Humility and grasp Peace.
~ Hildegard of Bingen

REASONS TO BE CONTENT

Number One: God brought me here. It is by His will that I am in this place. In that fact I will rest.

Number Two: He will keep me here in His love and give me grace to behave as His child.

Number Three: He will make the trial a blessing, teaching me the lessons He intends for me to learn and working in me the grace He means to bestow.

Number Four: In His good time He can bring me out again. How and when, He knows. So let me say I am here.

~Andrew Murray

Contentment is a pearl of great price,
and whoever procures it as the expense of ten
thousand desires makes a wise and happy choice.
~ John Balguy

*And I smiled to think God's greatness
flowed around our incompleteness,
round our restlessness His rest.*
~ Elisabeth Barrett Browning

*If you take little account of yourself,
you will have peace, wherever you live.
~ Abba Poemen*

The best things in life are nearest:
Breath in your nostrils, light in your eyes,
flowers at your feet, duties at your hand,
the path of right just before you.
Then do not grasp at the stars, but do life's
plain, common work as it comes, certain
that daily duties and daily bread are
the sweetest things in life.
~ Robert Lewis Stevenson

One who cannot find tranquility
from within, will search for it
in vain elsewhere.
~ La Rochefoucauld (adapted)

Prayer:
Lord, thank You for giving us the
possibility to be content whatever
our circumstances. Thank You
for those who love us and help us
to live in peace and joy. Help us to
see Your hand and trust in You
for all that we do. Amen.

175

Live in Love

He is not far from each one of us. For in Him
we live and move and exist, as even some of
your own poets have said, "For we are also
His offspring." Being God's offspring then, we
shouldn't think that the divine nature is like gold
or silver or stone, an image fashioned by human
art and imagination. (Acts 17:27–29)

If God is not far from you, if you are His child, then
He is intimately aware of all the details of your life.
He knows you and has even given you a portion of the
Divine nature. With that, He helps us to live in love.
He inspires us to give our best to those around us.

What does it mean to you to be God's child? Perhaps
it means that you view all of His children with more loving eyes. Perhaps it means that you
feel compassion toward those
who live in poverty of spirit
or of life's necessities.

As a person who lives in love, it certainly means that you respond to the desires and the needs of those within your sphere of influence. That may mean you are an excellent spouse or a great mother. It may mean that you are generous to the people who work for you, or that you recognize the light in others.

You have a calling on your life, to rise and shine and make the world a better place, embracing the good, giving what you can and leading with your heart. It is how you achieve the greatest joy. Live in love today. Be your Father's heavenly child!

> Live in the world as if
>   God and your soul only were in it,
>   that your heart may be captive
>   to no earthly thing.
>   ~John of the Cross

How far you go in life depends on
your being tender with the young,
compassionate with the aged,
sympathetic with the striving,
and tolerant of the weak and strong.
Because someday in your life
you will have been all of these.
~ George Washington Carver

Love, all alike,
no season knows, nor clime,
Nor hours, days, months, which are
the rags of time.
~ John Donne

The pain of emotional
trials and worries can
almost always be lessened
by a little love.
~ Chris Edwards

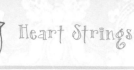

LOVE TIPS

For attractive lips, speak words of
   kindness.

For beautiful eyes, see the good in other
   people.

To lose weight, let go of stress and the
   need to control others.

To improve your ears, listen for God's
   voice in every conversation.

Touch someone each and every day
   with your love.

Count your blessings, and step back
   from the thorns of life.

For greater strength, lift the spirits of
   those around you.

For a stronger heart, hug others and
   offer forgiveness.

Try more faith and less worry.

Follow your path of life, embrace others
   along the way, or carve a new trail
   for others to follow.

Walk in love and love others as God has
   loved you.

~Karen Moore

Prayer:

Lord, sometimes it feels like we miss the point of living. We miss the fact that we are made in Your image and that we were designed in love, for love, and to create more love in this world. Help us to live in love and embrace all that it means to be kinder and more loving human beings. We ask this in the name of Your beloved Son, Jesus. Amen.

Heart Strings

Light My Fire

I will arise now and go about the city, through the streets and the plazas. I will seek the one I love. I sought him, but did not find him. The guards who go about the city found me. I asked them. "Have you seen the one I love?" I had just passed them when I found the one I love. I held on to him and would not let him go. (Song of Songs 3:2–4)

The very nature of love is its gift to cause a flame to grow in the heart. It ignites on the first recognition that it's there and spends itself over time. With nurture and encouragement, the flame dies down, but never goes out. No matter how long it burns, it lights an incredible fire of joy.

Whether you imagine the love you have for your spouse, or the continual seeking of God for His beloved children, the flame of love is intentional. It seeks to find the object of its affection. Love expresses itself in passionate embraces and determined effort to keep it fulfilled and sustained.

"Have you seen the one I love?" is a quest and a question that we have all been on somewhere in our journey. Be sure that God has the answer. In you, He sees the one He loves.

Spirit-filled souls are ablaze for God. They love with a love that glows. They serve with a faith that kindles. They serve with a devotion that consumes. They hate sin with fierceness that burns. They rejoice with a joy that radiates. Love is perfected in the fire of God. ~ Samuel Chadwick

No erudition, no purity of diction, no width of mental outlook, no flowers of eloquence, no grace of person can atone for lack of fire. Prayer ascends by fire. Flame gives prayer access as well as wings, acceptance as well as energy. There is no incense without fire no prayer without flame. ~ E. M. Bounds

Enthusiasm is as good a thing in the Church as fire is in a cook stove.
~Billy Sunday

All God can give us is his love and this love
becomes tangible—a burning of the soul—
it sets us on fire to the point of
forgetting ourselves.
~ Brother Roger

Prayer:
Lord, You know that the most
beautiful thing in the world is for us
to take our passion for You and for
each other to a greater level. We
have to keep our fire lit so that we
can share that warmth and that
light with those around us. Keep us
ever close to You, the Source of the
true Light that glows in our hearts.
Amen.

Love's Prayer

*Pour out your heart like water before
the Lord's presence. (Lam. 2:19)*

Nothing causes the heart to fill up to over-flowing
like love. It floods the soul with its presence and washes
over the spirit. It can totally change the course of your
life direction. Love is a force to be reckoned with and
needs to be handled with prayer.

Every kind of love, whether it's a person who stole
your heart when you were young, or your child, or your
puppy, brings value and joy to your life. Prayer protects
love and gives you a place to pour out your heart like
water in both joy and sorrow.

Pray for those you love. Pray for more love to know
them even better than you do now. Pray for opportunities
to allow your love to overflow in
each other's daily lives. Pray
that the love you share
will be a treasure for
all time.

187

God celebrates every experience of love you have and wants nothing more than for you to continue in love, offering it up to Him in prayer and praise. Thank God, that He is the author of all that brings love into this world. When you pour out your heart to Him in prayer for your loved ones, He is ready to listen and give you peace.

When you can't put your prayers into words, God hears your heart.
~ Unknown Author

If you are swept off your feet,
it's time to get on your knees.
~ Fred Beck

Prayer opens the heart to God, and it is the means by which the soul, though empty, is filled by God.
~ John Bunyan

Real prayer comes not from gritting your teeth, but from falling in love.
~ Richard Foster

YOU ARE LOVE'S PRAYER

You breathe,
You sigh,
You send a prayer
To the heavens,
To the God of your heart.
You inhale the day,
And exhale the night,
Comforted by the light of hope
That stays forever in your soul.
You pour out your heart,
To the One who sees you,
Who knows you
And who calls you by name.
Love is a prayer of continual hope.
Let peace
Overflow your heart today.
~Karen Moore

He prayeth best, who loveth best
All things both great and small
For the dear God who loveth us,
He made and loveth all.
~ Samuel Taylor Coleridge

Certain thoughts are prayers. There are moments
when whatever be the attitude of the body,
the soul is on its knees. ~ Victor Hugo

Take God for your spouse and friend and walk
with him continually, and you will not sin and will
learn to love, and the things you must do will work
out prosperously for you. ~ John of the Cross

There is nothing that causes us to love
others so much, as praying for them.
~ William Law (adapted)

We must know God before we can love. In order
to know God, we must often think of Him and
when we come to love Him, we shall then also
think of Him often, for our hearts will be with
our treasure. ~ Brother Lawrence (adapted)

Prayer:
Lord, You have taught us to love others and to pray for one another. You have offered us a way to have intimate conversation with You about all matters of the heart. You see our hearts and listen to our hopes and fears and desires. Thank You for loving us so much and giving us a way to talk to You about the people and the things which concern us the most. Amen.

Slings and Arrows of Love

Be at peace among yourselves. And we exhort you, brothers: warn those who are irresponsible, comfort the discouraged, help the weak, be patient with everyone. See to it that no one repays evil for evil to anyone, but always pursue what is good for one another and for all. (1 Thess. 5:13–15)

Cupid's arrow sometimes hits the mark. We fall deeply in love with someone and they reciprocate. All is well. We cannot imagine anything more pure and wonderful than the love we feel.

Sometimes though, Cupid's arrow simply pierces our hearts and leaves us with the ache and pain and disappointment of love. When that happens, we have to make choices. We have to come to God in prayer and trust Him to guide us through the difficult paths ahead, deeply rutted with dreams shattered as love walked away.

Most of us have been disappointed by the experience of love. That kind of fracture can even happen in the best of friendships, because love is not perfect. Perfect love exists in God alone.

If it's time for you to move on from the pitfalls of the past, the love experiences that went awry, then offer your heart to God in prayer. Thank Him for the opportunity you had to participate in love and to learn from love and then allow yourself to breathe in His love.

After time passes, His love will renew your spirit and heal your heart. His love will guide you again to a place where love resides. One broken arrow does not mean that you are out of love. Open your heart and love will wing its way to you, heal the disappointment and the hurt, and offer you sweet joy.

Faith is often strengthened right at the place of disappointment.
~Rodney McBride

"Hope" is the thing with feathers—
That perches in the soul—
And sings the tunes without the words—
And never stops—at all.
~ Emily Dickinson

We love to expect,
and when expectation is either
disappointed or gratified, we want to
be again expecting.
~ Samuel Johnson

We must accept
finite disappointment,
but we must never
lose infinite hope.
~ Martin Luther King Jr.

Know this: though love is weak and hate is
strong, yet hate is short, and love is long.
~ Kenneth Boulding

*The way to love anything
is to realize that it might be lost.*
~ G. K. Chesterton

The soul that walks in love neither
tires others nor grows tired.
~ John of the Cross

*The perfectionist ethic of Jesus
demands that love be poured forth
whether or not we suffer from injustice.*
~ Reinhold Neibuhr

Only love enables humanity to grow,
because love engenders life
and it is the only form of energy
that lasts forever.
~ Michel Quoist

Prayer:
Lord, sometimes we're disappointed by the people we love. Sometimes we disappoint the people who love us. Help us to forgive each other when we do foolish things that cause hearts to break. Remind us of Your unconditional love for us that gives us the room to grow and make mistakes and come back again to Your embrace. In Jesus' name. Amen.

In Love and Friendship

A friend loves at all times. (Prov. 17:17)

Love and friendship seem like they go hand in hand. After all, we like to think the person we've picked as a partner through life thinks of us as a friend. If you stepped back from your partner to assess the level of your friendship, what might you find? Where do the ideals of love and friendship meet?

We may not be able to create a manifesto on friendship here, but we might realize a few of the things that friends value in each other. Friendships are often built around these kinds of things:

- Mutual admiration and respect
- A love for similar activities
- Knowing that you can share matters of the heart fully and deeply
- Loving the moments when you can laugh together for no reason at all

- Enjoying the sense of peace that being together brings
- Sharing a faith for the God of the Universe
- Mutual affection
- Being there for each other like no one else can be
- Comforting, caring, supporting each other's dreams

These are just a few of the things that make you good partners. They're also some of the things that make you great lifelong friends. Let your partner know how much it means to you to share your incredible friendship.

What is a friend?
A single soul dwelling in two bodies.
~ Aristotle

Sometimes being a friend means
mastering the art of timing. There is a
time for silence. A time to let go and
allow people to hurl themselves into their
own destiny. And a time to prepare to pick
up the pieces when it's all over.
~ Octavia Butler

Blessed is the influence
of one true, loving soul on another.
~ George Eliot

Life is to be fortified by
many friendships. To love
and be loved is the greatest
happiness of existence.
~ Sydney Smith

NO ONE QUITE LIKE YOU

There's no one quite like you,
To make me laugh out loud,
No one else when I do well,
Who makes me feel so proud.

There's no one quite like you
When life just gets me down,
Who picks me up to start again
And chase away a frown.

There's no one quite like you
Who knows just what to say,
When I feel lost or so confused
By things life brings my way.

The light of love shines brightly
In each thing you say and do,
Thanks for loving me, my Friend,
There's no one quite like you!
~Karen Moore

202

Two are better than one because they have a good reward for their efforts. For if either falls, his companion can lift him up; but pity the one who falls without another to lift him up. Also, if two lie down together, they can keep warm; but how can one person alone keep warm? And if somebody overpowers one person, two can resist him. A cord of three strands is not easily broken. (Eccl. 4:9–12)

A friend is a person
with whom I may be sincere.
Before him, I may think aloud.
~ Emerson

By friendship you mean
the greatest love,
the greatest usefulness,
the most open
communication,
the noblest sufferings,
the severest truth,
the heartiest counsel,
and the greatest union of minds
of which brave men and women
are capable.
~ Jeremy Taylor

True friends don't spend time gazing into each
other's eyes. They may show great tenderness
towards each other, but they face in the same
direction toward common projects, goals,
above all, towards a common Lord.
~ C. S. Lewis

Prayer:
Lord, there's certainly no one quite
like You and we're awed by Your
friendship and love and presence
in our lives. Thank You for blessing
us beyond measure with people who
can help us sort out life, comfort
us in sorrow, and shine a light on
our pathway. Amen.

Unstrung, Undone, Simply Stung... by Love!

He heals the brokenhearted and binds up their wounds. He counts the number of the stars; He gives names to all of them. Our Lord is great, vast in power; His understanding is infinite. The LORD helps the afflicted and brings the wicked to the ground. (Ps. 147:3–6)

It's happened to all of us. We've been weaving together the fabric of love and everything seems glorious. We know that somehow this time, things are different and that this love will last forever.

Then, somehow, before we were even able to put all the pieces of the relationship together, things start unraveling at the seams.

We're being pulled apart one fiber at a time. It's taken the beautiful piece we made and very little remains.

What do we do? Heartbreak is its own kind of sorrow. It means that something we hoped for is lost. It means that prayers we thought were answered are no longer viable. It simply shakes our world.

Remember that when you hurt, when you suffer any kind of heartbreak, your Lord suffers with you. He knows you and calls you by name. He sees you and seeks to bind your wounds. When you're feeling all unstrung, turn to Him and let Him hold you close. He always loves you and is always ready to embrace you even when heartbreak enters in. Draw close to God and He will draw close to you.

Sorrow looks back,
worry looks around,
but faith looks up.
~Author Unknown

We are tossed on a tide
that puts us to the proof,
and if we could not sob our
troubles in your ear, what hope
should we have left to us?
~ Augustine of Hippo

Our trusting the Lord does not mean
that there are not times of tears.
I think it is a mistake as Christians to
act as though trusting the Lord and
tears are not compatible.
~ Francis Schaeffer

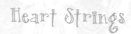

Give no place to despondency.
This is a dangerous temptation
of the adversary. Melancholy
contracts and withers the heart.
~ Madame Guyon

Whatever is true, whatever is honor-
able, whatever is just, whatever is pure,
whatever is lovely, whatever is commend-
able—if there is any moral excellence
and if there is any praise—dwell on these
things. (Phil. 4:8)

Prayer:
Thank You for drawing close to us when our hearts are broken. We are humbled that we can put all of our joys and sorrows before You and that You love and honor us so much, You're willing to hear those things that grieve our spirits and cause us sadness. Lift us up, Lord, when we cannot pick ourselves up. Grant us Your grace and mercy and peace no matter what happens to us, no matter how much of life seems to fall apart. Keep us in faith and love by Your side always. Amen.

The Alpha and Omega of Love

I am the Alpha and the Omega, the First and the Last, the Beginning and the End. (Rev. 22:13)

The wonderful thing about love is that it is all around us. Like sunshine, it permeates the world in almost any place we choose to look. All it takes to see it is an attitude that embraces all that love can be. Since we know that the only reason we actually love anyone or anything is because God loved us first and invited us into a relationship with Him. He is always ready to teach us more about what love means and how we can realize even more love in our lives.

God is the author of love. He truly wrote the best book on the subject that will ever be written. He sees each of us from the inside out, looking directly at our hearts to see what motivates our thoughts and moves us to act. All that we come to know of love is nothing in comparison to what we can know.

As you imagine love, as you look at how love has been expressed to you and how it has played out in your life, think again about what you want from love now, in this moment of your life. How do you want to express love to your spouse, or your children? How do you want to leave a legacy of love to the world so that it is truly a better place because you were here? Your God will be with you always. His love is eternal. His love is unconditional. The beauty of His love is that He gives it in continual abundance. He makes it new for us every morning. He pumps love through our hearts and minds in the same way that He gives us air to breathe.

Wherever love has taken you so far, it's not the end. In fact, it will never end for all the love you share on earth, will be love that moves from one generation to the next. You will have made a difference just by being the ambassador of God's love. One thing to keep in mind is that there's always more room at the inn, always room for love to be born in your heart.

Shout "Hallelujah!" for love! Live in joy eternal. Walk in love!

The moment you wake up each morning,
all your wishes and hopes for the day
rush at you like wild animals.
And the first job each morning consists
in shoving it all back in listening to that
other voice, taking that other point of view,
letting that other, larger, stronger,
quieter life come flowing in.
~ C. S. Lewis

Knowing that I am not the one in control
gives great encouragement. Knowing the
One who is in control is everything.
~ Alexander Michael

Purity of heart means to
love God above all things
and at the same time to see him
everywhere in all things.
~ Teilhard de Chardin

215

God loves us not because of who we are,
but because of who He is!
~ Unknown Author

For the love of God is broader
Than the measures of man's mind
And the heart of the Eternal
Is most wonderfully kind.
~ F. W. Faber

Love to Jesus is the basis of all true piety,
and the intensity of this love will ever be the
measure of our zeal for His glory. Let us love
Him with all our hearts, and then diligent labor,
and consistent living will be sure to follow.
~ C. H. Spurgeon

In his love, he clothes us,
enfolds us and embraces
us that tender love
completely surrounds us,
never to leave us.
~ Julian of Norwich

Prayer:
Father of love and life, We are truly thankful for all You do to teach us to love one another. You loved us before we were even born, and You will love us into eternity. Nothing surpasses Your love. Please help us to share that kind of everlasting and unconditional love with our families and friends. Help us to be good students, anxious to learn more about how to love You and others with our whole heart and mind. Help us to always reach out in joy and shine your light on those around us. In Jesus' name we pray. Amen.

Dear Readers,

Thank you for sharing your heartstrings, playing the music of love to all the people who are dear to you. Thank you for wanting more of the kind of loving relationships that God truly wants you to have. Follow His example and love will blossom and grow for you. The more you give love, the more you receive and so your cup will truly overflow.

The God of your heart sees you and knows you and you are always His priority.

Feel His love, radiate His joy and keep letting your life play with sentimental heartstrings. The music will be beautiful.

God loves you always. May His love shine on you and bless you each day.

~Karen Moore